The Singing Mountain

Elisabeth Cooper

Dedication

This book is for the seekers, for the lovers of beauty and mystery, for the wonderstruck warriors who never stop living for the King of the Mountain.

This book is for the poets. Your time has come. Release your hearts into the world and watch as the eyes of the earth turn to see you; as the hearts of the nations transform under the beauty, truth, and power of your words.

And, finally, this book is for my friends and family who have fiercely loved and supported me. You know who you are. You are gold to me.

Contents

Munificent
Rivers
God Marches
Woven
Remembrance
Unbound
Heritage
The Sound
Words Drawn
Ascending
Untethered

Spoken Word (Adapted for Print):

Calling the Artists
Where Poets Prophesy
Wake the Dead

A Note from the Author

Dear Reader,

I am so honored that you've picked up my book.

I am convinced that poetry is more than mere words on a page, more than an optional addition to our literary consumption. Good poetry contains deep truths, allows us to gaze into a pool of beauty and truth if we take the time to listen as it speaks.

The potential of poet and poetry has been grossly underestimated. A poet is more than a craftsman. Poetry is more than pretty words.

A poet is one who translates the loveliness of truth and goodness into something that awakens new ways of understanding. Poetry flows from the poet's heart as something the world can stop and marvel at, something that can move hearts to the point of healing and change, something that can shift society and culture into the arms of justice.

Poetry should speak with eloquence and authority. It should hold and unfold mysteries. It should prophesy and create.

My greatest hope for this collection is that it lives up to that standard, that it opens the door to more for your heart, and that it takes you out of time and into eternity. I hope that in your quiet moments these words become portals into the reality of dimensions beyond what you see and that you are transported into realms of beauty, truth, revelation, and healing as you read.

This book is for seekers. May it be a blanket of comfort and healing, a revealer of mysteries, a voice of wisdom.

May the light of these words illuminate darkness, and may this volume become a friend to your heart,

Elisabeth

Zion

Zion

We carved our hearts
In the mountain sound

And the sound of the mountain
Carved its heart in us

Imprinted with words
Of thundering drums

Surrounded by light
Dancing strings wildly

Ringing

Voices of bells
Announcing freedom

Air awash with music
Colors alive with Wisdom

Zion has a hold on me
The Music of this city is home to me

I'm caught in patterns of the mountain's light
Finding lost memories
Of before
My before

In folds and crevices
Valleys and peaks

I have come to find
Where I was born

In the dream of a King
Washed in wonder and possibility

The hues of Zion
In the city of my heart

Everlast

I'm in the city
And the city is in me

Identity carved
In waters deep

Deep mountain waters
Sing with fire, wine, and oil

Born in blood and water
In the rhythm of His heartbeat
I remember
My origin

Zion singing

Mountain

I saw a mountain

    with worlds inside

And the sound of
gardens blooming
swept over me like music

A teeming creation

    of spices and fruit

        cities upon cities

           doorways to universes

Libraries and scribes

pour out living letters
filling mouths with
Wonder and Justice

Patterns of Grace
weave reality into
atmospheres higher
than heights of earth

The Mountain sings,

    forever new and ancient

      the songs of Holy

        an invitation

We Build Cities

Let dreams of God
from heights of Zion
pour out like water
into the earth
from the fountain of
our lives.

We build cities
the earth has never seen.

From inside the glow of
the singing mountain
they rise in our hearts
to form

Cities born of
blueprints
stored in dreams
of Your heart.

They wait

for hearts to believe
beyond the reach
of what they've seen.

Minds

to open up to eternal beauty
waking the future today.

Eyes

with new cities in their view
glory carved from Zion, deep

Time

Healers

Wisdom is better than silver and gold
Saturate with substance
I cannot hold in my hands

Call me a new name the earth has never heard
I'll ride on the wings of Justice
Bearing the unuttered miracle
Wielding healing
Inside the burned-out broken cracks of creation

Give me a drink from the ancient well
While whispers ignite fires
The dawn summons me

Where are the healers of time?

Governors

The arches and concaves of time
That bend, buckle, break
Under the weight of reality
And the government of wine

This malleable substance

    Time

Begs to be governed
By sons and daughters

Take it in your hands

    Grace

Like the forming
Of earth's clay

Quantum Garden

Remember past your present
A quantum garden
A shining city

The reality of life is
More firmly rooted
In the unseen

More ordered
Beyond the confines
Of time and space

Outside of time
Into eternity

Your life is bigger
Than you once thought

History's Future

To take what's been done and heal it
Is not so out of reach

The arms of eternity
Override the confines of time

And Grace drips on fissures
Of the long lost and broken

Never let time stare you down
Or defeat you

Its ability to govern lies only
In the permission you grant it

Blood cries out for justice
Death will never win

Healing runs over forgotten places
The future is changed to promise

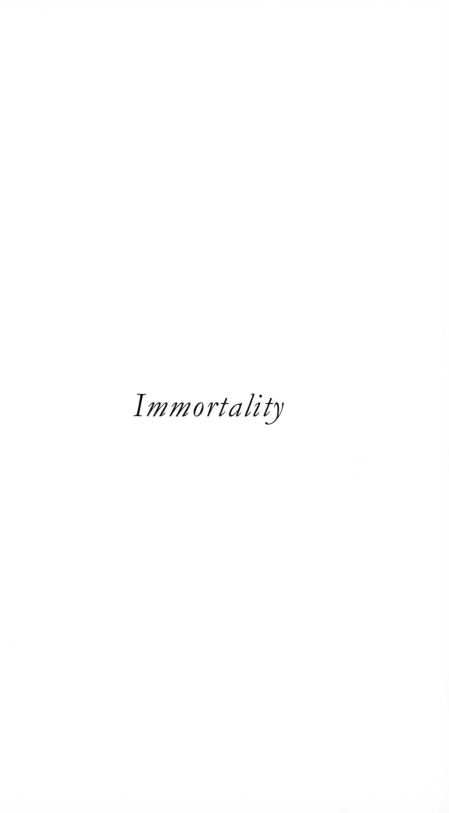

Immortality

Bearers of Life

We bend light with our words;

> draw grace over darkness,
> pull fire into monotony of days,
> bring thunder to break injustice.

We are the shifters
the shapers
the makers.

> We are the breakers of death,
> born of the Breaker of Death.

> We are the carriers
> the bearers
> the vessels

> of

> Life.

Movement

Movement is
opposed to death

Blood pumping
water rushing
sound dancing

Symphony
of Breath

Take
one
more
breath

And another
and another
again
repeat

The refrain of immortality

Streams of Consciousness

In golden rivulets
Connecting and dissecting
Dimensions
Alive here
Alive everywhere

Light has no shore
Breath has no limit
Outside of time

Mysteries from shattered cubes
Come clattering
Over false perceptions

Until broken, they lie
Under a sea of Grace

And a River that lives
To breathe life
In streams of consciousness

Concentric waves
Beyond banks
Of time and place

The Substance of Grace

The substance of grace
Liquid time
Like holy wine

Rises under me
Wings and tides
Song and rhyme

Grace

Breaking of ground
Thunder of the sound

Justice

Carrying, lifting
Weighing, sifting

The empowerment of the ages
In the substance of grace

Over me

Voice of the Mystic

Mystic

Let the nations hear
The voice of the mystic
Creation listens
Fire glistens
In mysteries mined and traversed
By the brave in the earth

Hidden they've lived
Until the earth makes a final appeal

Crying out for golden threads of understanding
To spin around them
Like the firesong of angels

Calling for the substance of flames, oil, wine
Desperate for wisdom and meaning

We've turned all our lives
On this revolving axis
But we failed to live revolution

So the voice of the mystic comes
Silence, singing, sound
Shaking the ground of cracked foundations
To build with sure revelation
The quantum glory

The voice of the mystic cries
Make way for union
In whirlwinds of words
And tips of tongues
Articulating holy fire

Realms

I came up
through
a flaming sword
swirling with letters
of light.

I came up
through
a singing river
breathing air of water
at rest.

I came up
through
a golden garden
a fortress
of a name.

Fires and spirals
took me in their arms
carrying me into
unbreakable might

A fountain of unceasing love

Remembering

Somewhere
deep in the river of our blood
we remember
Eden

Generation upon generation
of forgotten grace
but the winds of Eden
still blow

Light in my veins
the fire awakens
nearer to me than
air in my lungs

Realities dream

To awaken Eden
in corners
of my heart
asleep to the Light

Flames of Wisdom

Sit with Wisdom
until her counsel covers you

Steadily singing
until night
gives up its stand
against you

And winds
are no longer
monstrous beasts

But wild still
they burn with fire

Galaxies

Awaken to wonder
and cavernous depths
of infinite breath
alive in me

Firebolt

Awaken to lighting
striking
each cell blazing
with light

Singing

I am eternal depth
nations and worlds
I am one with the Timeless
Limitless

Heart

The only timepiece of heaven
constant rhythm
perfect order
pumping light

River

The world is about to see
galaxies in me

Endless

In endless cords of light
Refracting white
Eternal color
Time does not imprison
Distance is an illusion

The mystic reaches
Beyond time and space
Lives beyond reason
Where reason was born

Deep in the embrace
Of Reality

Kaleidoscope

Seven flames combined
as I looked into
bright mantles
of Holy

Mingled fire dancing
as I stood upon
a lucid sea
of Actuality

And now I see
everything
as it is intended

Gushing from
fiery hues
of Spirit burning

Sacred

Listening is holy
Observing, sacred

Fires
and
rivers
tell

The holiness
of listening
carries
wonder
and
understanding

In hands
held
open
amid
thunder
and winds

The Music of Stillness

There is a philosophy of progress
Nothing grows in stillness

We must keep moving
Make things happen

Turn the cogs of the wheels of machines
Sweat and toil and churn

To that I say
Go stand in a forest

Let purposeful stillness
Seep into your bones

Absorb life in holy serenity
The progress of rest
For in silence
There is music

In stillness
There is growth

The mighty trees are about their business

Without sweat
With effortless grandeur

As they forge life in stillness

They sing
They live
They grow
They stand

Carpets of moss
Ferns with their swords
Wild hearted blooms

They sing
They live
They grow
They stand

The forest and the wilderness know
The unending well of the mystics

Enfolded and captured
They rest unto greatness

In stillness running with rivers of music

In stillness wrought with growth and strength

In stillness bursting with banquets of beauty

They sing
They live
They grow
They stand

Hearts of Fire and Steel

Bring back the fervid zeal
The hearts of fire and steel
Hands that believe and build

Bring back words of silk and hammers
Spirits in light crafted
Minds of wisdom and wing-spread

Let the promise of beyond what we see
Awaken
Origin of Breath, blow

In embers and winds of Eden
We wake to the glow

Who are These People?

The Kainos people
The tomorrow people
Today
The cloud walkers
The living-well talkers
The wine cellar dwellers
Immortal

With honey dripping from their tongues
With mantles of eloquence
Resting on their shoulders

Who are these people?!

The dark horses
The special forces
The people with divine DNA
Coursing through their veins

The Heart of the Mystic

Hands

    Reaching

Grasping mysteries

    To hold before the eyes of nations

Earth, behold.

    Cosmos, hold your breath.

The mystics,

    Living in winds

    Walking on clouds

Inviting mysteries to dance in our veins

And we, in the veins of mystery

Right outside the matrix

    Beyond the fringes

    Of the comprehensible known

Lives the mystic

Reaching

    Dwelling

    Breathing the air of the unseen

        The revelator

Dreaming

    Leaning

      Abiding in eternal mystery

Earth, listen

    Cosmos, at attention

The rustle of a lion rising

The lilt of a turtledove singing

Carried on the voice of the mystics

    Chariot songs

The mystic cries

    The mystery is reality

John, the revelator cries

    Look, listen

        The glistening dawn

        Of dreams unseen

Combing through

words of silver wisdom

    And melodies soft and loud

New Poetry

New poetry is crying out
from hidden caves
from city fountains
from the mountain of Light

Colors on words we've never seen
frequency gleaming in syllables untethered
from mortal logic

Guttural cries for redemption, reason
transcendent replies from
wells deep and wide

Listen

    Order from chaos

        Everything alive

            Wakened to the sound

Listen

   Justice runs swiftly

      Into nations and systems

         Transformation all around

Beauty rests

upon hearts who stop to listen

    The mystics

      The poet prophets

        Rising

Light Sings

Where-forever I go
Light sings
In choruses great
In whispering winds
Covered in soft and furious strength

Walking encompassed
By feathered wings
Courageous words
Build seas of power in me

I walk inside layers
Worlds and cities
Of endless light

Justice

Where Justice Lives

There's a sound of rumbling
The thunder of laughter
In the courts

And all the chariots of justice ride
On the rhythm

Joy, the sound of government
Swirling around in the wine

Profound
Justice lives
In waves and breakers
Of life and light
In body and blood

In the redemption of time
In mines of destiny
Where the treasure
Holds
Ancient wisdom

Where light
Sounds its trumpet
And life prevails

Crown

Justice
Turns its head
To tear-soaked hearts

Looks pain in the eye

Stares slavery and death
Down the barrel
Of a song
That crowns the head
Of the broken

A Song of Justice for the Farmer

Tears of God
mend the soil
as worn hands toil
to turn dirt into beauty
and perhaps bread

Unseen, forgotten by most
Beaten down by hands
who hold corrupt power
In places they've never stood

But higher arms hold noble hearts
The Highest of all
And the wind of justice blows
On dreams of Eden

For dirt is well loved
by the King
And from the beginning
It has held the song of His breath

God
was a gardener here
before He was a carpenter

The Great Cloud

David's Song

You heard the songs I played
for a king tormented

You saw raw grit held in a stone
strike a giant dead

You saw my strength
You saw a shining moment

I came out of the shadows that day

But you never heard the years of songs
I played in open fields

On dewy nights
on blazing mornings

Those hills are full of my song

The earth has heard
no other ear

Still my solace abides

There are some songs that drip with gold
and the mountains are their home

Listen to Sheerah

Authority rests on my frame
like a silken mantle of grace

I will not let my voice
remain tethered to
the age I live in

I am a woman

of incredulous audacity
and the world will hear me

Vision and Wisdom
I have
caught and held
to wield
and lay upon history
like bricks and mortar
unmovable

I build cities
I usher in the future

Listen

You can hear it

The sound of hammers and stone
foundations set and settling
they will remain unmoved
for thousands of years

God, Himself, defends my cities

Still, stands the sun
over them
to defeat
enemies at the gates

Listen to me-
Build your cities

From counsels
and mountain Light
come blueprints
for cities that will stand
and change the face of the earth
forever

Listen to me

Mary

No one expected Him to weep

My own tears consumed me
I knew who He was when I poured
All I had in this world at His feet

The Redeemer of all things

I thought death had swallowed my brother
Grief hung around my neck
I had one hope

Him

One would think the King of the Universe
Would first work the miracle
And then we'd rejoice

But the heart of a King
Sits with the broken
And my friend weeps with me

Warriors & Forerunners

Pioneers

Where are the pioneers
With dew and pearls of destiny
Laced between their lips

Calloused hands

Eyes that see beyond brushes of chaos
In the fire of His gaze they dwell
Becoming the blaze they behold

Fearless feet

Ears that hear beyond the clattering voices
Bellowing their cries of
Distraction, derailment, and deafening doubt

Unbending spines

Minds of steely oneness
In synchronicity with the thoughts of the King
Sword wielding wild spirits of the brave

Battle tested hearts

Proven in dark fiery silence
On roads they built alone
Graced in steadfast resolution

Fiercely forged

Unmoved in storms of accusation,
In the face of misunderstanding

Formed in solitary, wondrous paths of ancient
discovery

They stand

Hearts entangled into the King's rhythm
Taking shape in the sound of many waters
Love stronger than death

One

The earth has yet to hear the roar
Of the fire-branded warrior
Love driven revelators as they sound victory

Get ready

With voices of water and gavels
With hands of skill and beauty
With hearts of prophecy and fire

They come

Warrior

Night falls on the warrior
Rending eyes dim and heart heavy
Lending questions a bigger space than deserved
Pending answers in pools of uncertainty

When darkness
Brandishes time as a weapon
Still your heart

In the midst of the sound
You will hear
The stirring of waters and wind
Of thunder and rain

A fountainous song of everlasting love over you

And the song of love
Is the song of victory

Have you ever heard the drums of victory sound?
Like a force of reckoning and reigning
Like waves breaking
The rhythm shaking
Every voice contrary to the win

So now, my daring warrior
My rider of truth, my lover of justice
Let your bleeding heart sink safely
Into the rhythm of love and victory

Breathe
Breathe in
Breath out

And let
Your lungs fill

Let the shrill and vapid sound of defeat
Shatter to the ground

And let the Maker's hands hold you
The thundering drums of His heart surround

Consolation

Let Me bring you in
to rest a while
until all your tears
make a salty sea
and love comes in
like softness to win

Sit at My table
like a friend
at midnight calling
for grace and understanding

Come to the meadow
lay beside Me as stillness
moves the pain to leave

Let Me bring you in
I'll stand so you can fall
inside My heart tonight
and kindness isn't faith long forgotten

Run to the river
for healing in the water
stirring as doubt flees

Sit in My garden
where memories are planted
in the forgiving soil of justice

Silence

The absence of sound
Is not the silence I crave
But the absence of noise

Give me birdsong
And sighs of weary warriors
Pen scratch
And rivers speaking

Give me cries of honest hearts
A lone violin singing
Blossoms unfolding
Wind playing tips of pines

Give me laughter and tears
Give me boots on velvet earth
Give me crackling fires under silken skies

Give me the songs of purity and grace
Wonders that baptize

The Rumble

Where is that rumble coming from?
The earth is shifting
From deep wells come golden songs
Forged under wings
And carrying lightning

Where is that river running from?
Washing death and decay away
Rolling like thunder
From the throne of wonder
Symphonic release from the Conductor

Into living flames
And stones that breathe
The air of His heartbeat

Here are the hands that bear revolution
From mysteries come revelation
Graced in fertile soil
Of hearts in mystical union

Here are the hearts that will launch
The earth into the next era
Beyond revival
We come
Beyond history
We go
Into the new and ancient way
Of union revolution

This is the apocalypse now
This is the glory of a new age
This is the full revealing of Beauty

Tercets & Quatrains

Wisdom's Awakening

Drink the cup of Wisdom
Let her colors dance in your veins
Lightning meets thunder in the waking

Spun

Silver surrounds words of golden truth
And I am spun
In gleaming amber streams of honey

The Eyes of Justice

Justice rolls in wheels within wheels
And finally, eyes look upon
The forgotten

Before Time

Laughter and tears command the chariots of justice
And blood answered weeping blood
Before time saw its own face

Munificent

Munificent justice
A river kept teeming
By the reins of mercy

Rivers

Crooked made straight
In the rivers of my veins
From before the before

God Marches

The sound of thunder
Reverberates in the Balsam trees
God marches
And I am entangled into victory

Woven

In deep and ancient mystery I discover
Grace woven into life
And love breathing immortality

Remembrance

I shook slumber from my frame
Saw my reflection in eyes of fire
Suddenly I remembered
The dream I was born in

Unbound

Tears unbound
Brittle and brave
Held tight by wisdom
She spins her gold

Heritage

On the banks of provision
Beauty wept my eyes to see
And the red cord of heritage
Silken and singing- waits to baptize me

The Sound

My fingers run through the sound of justice
A racehorse at the gate
A turtledove singing

Words Drawn

Something deeper
Lives in words
Drawn from the river
Everlasting

Ascending

Realms
Like helix ladders
Ascending
Into mysteries of reality

Untethered

Untethered in concentric
Rhythms of grace
Above the circle of the earth
Cloudwalkers

*Spoken Word
(Adapted for Print)*

Calling the Artists

Wisdom has bellowed in the winds of the earth.
Joy has called out in longing.

Come!

Be the thunder of God in the earth.
Be the beauty of His name poured out.

I join my voice
with the voice like the sound of many waters,
the voice like the sound of a trumpet.

And I call for awakening

Silence the singers to truly sing.

Still the dancers
to dance the dance of divine romance
and rejoicing that crushes injustice.

Awaken the dreamers to dream
the dreams of heaven's heart.

Oh, you creators created by The Creator,
still yourselves
to receive the movement of heaven.
Silence yourselves to receive the sound of heaven.

Awaken yourself from sleep.
Come back to yourselves.
Come back to original design.

The great voice of loving-kindness is in the earth
again, the sound of the bridegroom come.

So come!

Come one, come all to the revolution,
to the great awakening,
to the spectacle of the ages.

Release the dancers!
The earth is groaning!
Give me your painters,
give me your poets,
give me your mathematicians and your magicians,
give me your musicians,
give me your downtrodden passionate lovers of
beauty.

Give me the fullness of a generation on its knees.

Give me the artists who sit in wisdom.

Give
them
to
me

and let their freedom be wrought
in the river of Life.
Let them be born again in the blood of covenant.

And then-
let the earth be shaken to its cultural core.

and let the government of joy and freedom come
bubbling up from the ancient wells.

Let the artists uncap the ancient wells!

We dig
We see
We hear

Let the poetry of promise pry open the depths of
healing for ancient wounds.

Let the beauty we make with our hands shape the
future into glory.

Let the sounds of our awakening shake brokenness-

like
the breaking of chains,
like
the crumbling of stone,
like
the rumbling of waves and breakers.
Like the waking of veins
that pump the blood and the wine
into dry bones on a desert floor.

Dancing.

Let the dry bones dance again.

Let streams flow in the desert.

This is the day, this is the hour for awakening
ushered forth in the arms of beauty and power.

This is your day.
This is your hour.

Let the artists loose-
The wild, unbridled, untamed, uninhibited

Let
them
loose

and watch constructs of religion crumble.

A new day is dawning.

So rise up and ring the bells of the morning,

all you people of beauty and wonder.

We are the song of a new day.

Where Poets Prophesy

Out in the wilderness

where poets prophesy to dead bones.

Out in the desert where a cry rings out.

Deep in the silence
where a call goes out to the four winds.

Tucked in the cave of darkness
there's a holy light.

These are the birthing rooms of miracles.

Nobody sees.

Nobody sees what happens in the darkness,
nobody sees the tears in the silence.

Nobody sees.

But these are the birthing rooms of miracles.
These are the places where seeds are planted.

These-

Are the dance floors of love,
The trading floors
where the catalysts for change are set like flint.

Immovable.

These are the corridors of power, the halls of
wonder, the chambers of thunder.

But

These

Are the places we never want to go,
the places we never want to know.

We don't want to be here,
we don't know how to see here.

These are the places we feel lost.
We question who we are here.

We

Question

Everything

And we must

For when we question, we find answers.

These

Are the incubators for destiny,
formation chambers of power,
the fierce establishers of authority.

These are sending rooms for miracles,
the places where the call rings out,
the rings are handed out.

Place the ring on my finger

and let its seal mark my life.

In the silence.
In the darkness.
In the wilderness.
In the desert.

These are the places we never want to go.

We don't want to go
and we most certainly don't want to stay.

But these are the places
where the light is born into darkness.

These are the places
where deep calls unto deep.

Deep. Calls. Unto. Deep

And we go there!

We go there
because we are the tomorrow people.
We are the dreamers of dreams.
We are the runners
in the foreground of the great unknown.
We are the pioneers and engineers of the future.
We are the creators of beauty,
the believers of justice and peace.
We are the priests and kings and prophets emerging
from the unknown depths of God.

We have been forged in pain and pressure.
We have been formed in fire, water, wine, and oil.
We have been found in the eyes of God.

We know the secret to the power of love.

Power lies in the places people never want to go.
Miracles are waiting.

They're waiting.

They're waiting.

They're waiting.

They're seeds on the winds of the wilderness
and they are waiting!

All the power of love we search for
is so often found in the places we never want to go.

But seek and you will find.

Seek, move, never relent.
Be brave, be strong, be courageous.

Forge into the deepest and highest place.

Even if you go alone,

Go.

For these are the dance floors of love.

Wake the Dead

We need more wakers to wake the sleeping
We need the sleeping to rise

The call for revolution runs deep and wide
Revolutionaries, the earth calls for keeping

Where are the scribes
and the poets and the bards
Who lift songs of light in the night
And craft truth and wisdom into words

Healing on their lips
Carrying grace in their grips
Singing outside of time
To unheard rhyme

That sets new paces and wins races
To shift spaces into realms we've only seen through
laces
Of whispers as we sat inside the gates

We are the gates who have run through the door
And we run without stopping
We do not tire
We do not weary
We run and we sing and we never stop

To shake false rhythms
To break systems of corruption
To heal the weeping
And raise the sleeping dead

We come bringing justice
And dreaming dreams
Of Eden rising
And a city hemmed in by gems

It's time for a new day breaking
Light cannot be taken
By darkness
So sing singers
And tell poets
And play fingers on strings to bring glory

And let the holy explosion
Rumble
Let darkness crumble
In the wake of the warriors who cry love in the
streets
And speak the jarring truth
To heal the nations and creation

Listen!
The sound of beauty is rising
Ring the bells of justice and
Wake the dead
The day is new

Made in the USA
Columbia, SC
17 September 2021